Isis 001

Ramses III 002

003

004 the goddess Bast

005

the sacred Uraeus snake 006

007

a mummy 008

Sebek Kneph 009

a mummy 010

1

011   peasant women bringing tribute from villages

Ptah and crocodiles   012

013

lion sphinx with human head   014

015

Menq
016

funeral boat or Baris, with shrine
017

018

the goddess of truth and justice
019

a war chariot with bow cases
020

Mut   021

2

022

023

024

Sapt

025

two forms of the goddess Bast

026

Anuris, guardian of the lower world

027

028

four-wheeled hearse

029

women beating tambourines and the *darabooka* drum

030

031

3

032

military chief in a palanquin; attendant behind bears a buckler

033

sarcophagus with the goddess
Nut on the breast

034

035   sacred tamarisk of Osiris

036   blind singers

037

038

Thoth

039

040

041

042

043

044

a weeping woman embraces
her husband's mummy

045

046

two harps and another instrument

048

Xeper in his boat, ruling the spirits of Heliopolis

047

harps, one with four strings

049

a Sem priest leads the Sa-mer-f into the presence of the statue

050

051

ornamentation for a ceiling

052

053

054

Imouthos   Serqa (Selk)

057

055

Amset

056

058

059

an Ethiopian princess in a *plaustrum* drawn by oxen

060

garb of a son of Ramses III

061

062

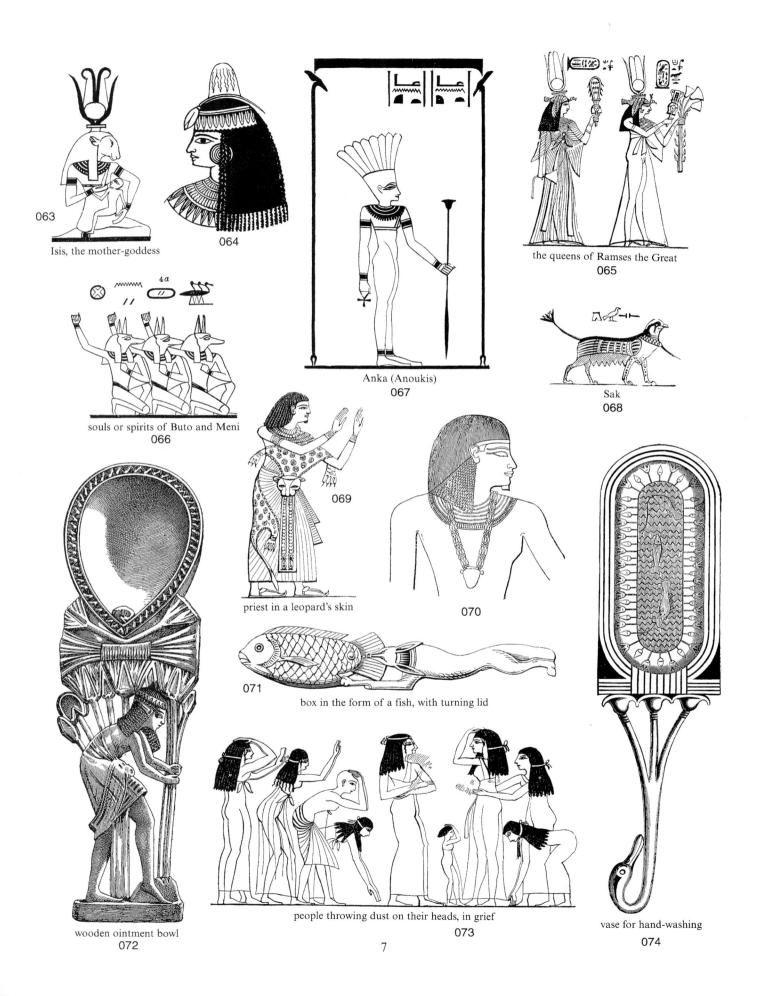

063

Isis, the mother-goddess

064

Anka (Anoukis)
067

the queens of Ramses the Great
065

souls or spirits of Buto and Meni
066

Sak
068

069

priest in a leopard's skin

070

071

box in the form of a fish, with turning lid

wooden ointment bowl
072

people throwing dust on their heads, in grief
073

vase for hand-washing
074

7

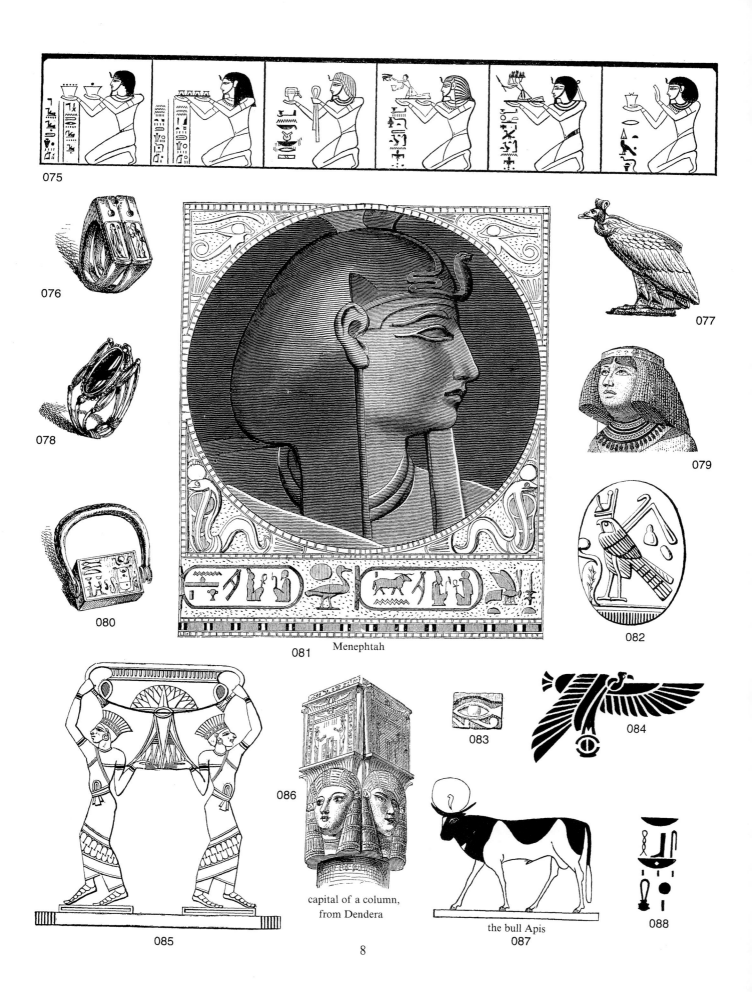

075

076

077

078

079

080

081
Menephtah

082

083

084

085

086
capital of a column,
from Dendera

087
the bull Apis

088

8

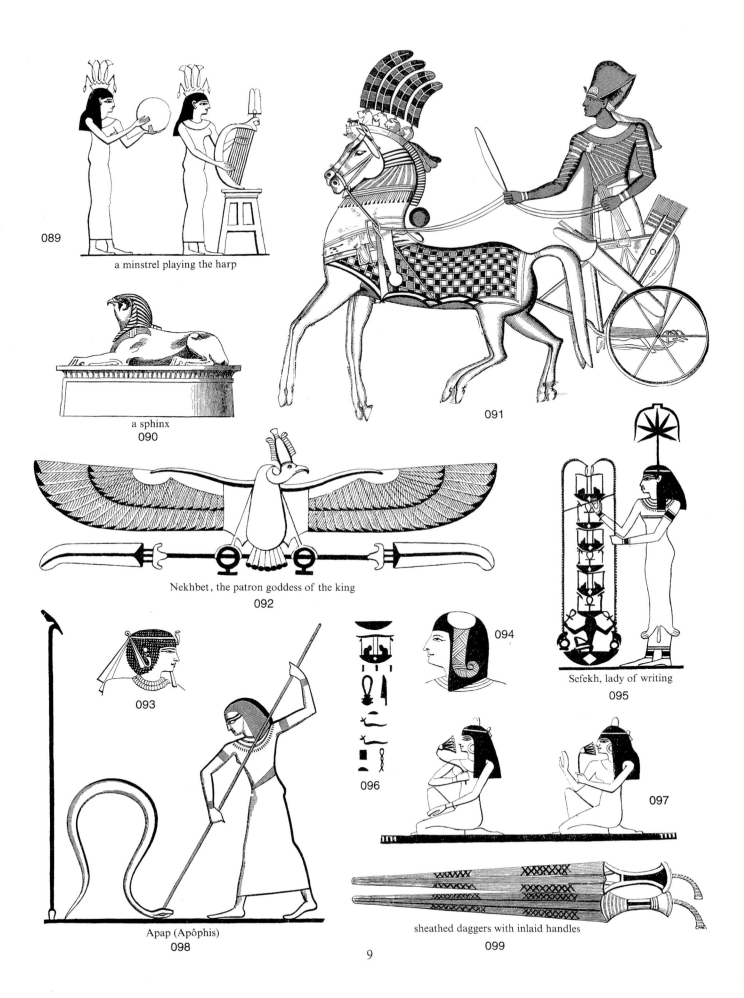

089

a minstrel playing the harp

a sphinx
090

091

Nekhbet, the patron goddess of the king
092

Sefekh, lady of writing
095

093

094

096

097

Apap (Apôphis)
098

sheathed daggers with inlaid handles
099

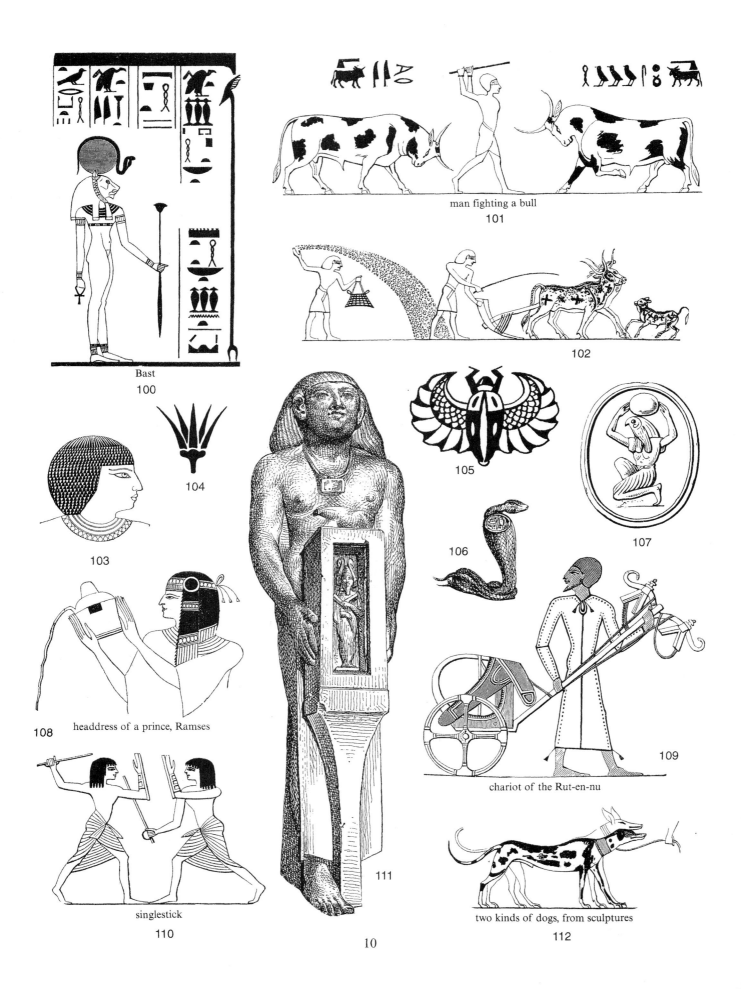

Bast
100

man fighting a bull
101

102

103

104

105

106

107

headdress of a prince, Ramses
108

109

chariot of the Rut-en-nu

111

singlestick
110

two kinds of dogs, from sculptures
112

Isis, Osiris, and Horus
113

114   the god Bes

115   Cleopatra

116

117

statue of Rui, a priest
118

Hathor as Ta-aha, "the cow,"
mother of Ra, "the Sun"
120

121

Isis suckling Horus
119

Horus spearing Apap (Apôphis)
122

11

123

125 vase with heads of gazelles and of horses

124 Isis

126

127 Axex

128

129

130

131

132

EICBAIT
EICAΘWPMI
ATWNBIAEIC
ΔEAKWPIXAIPE
ΠATEPKOCMOYXA
IPΘTPIMOPΦEΘEOC

133

Mentu-ra 134

12

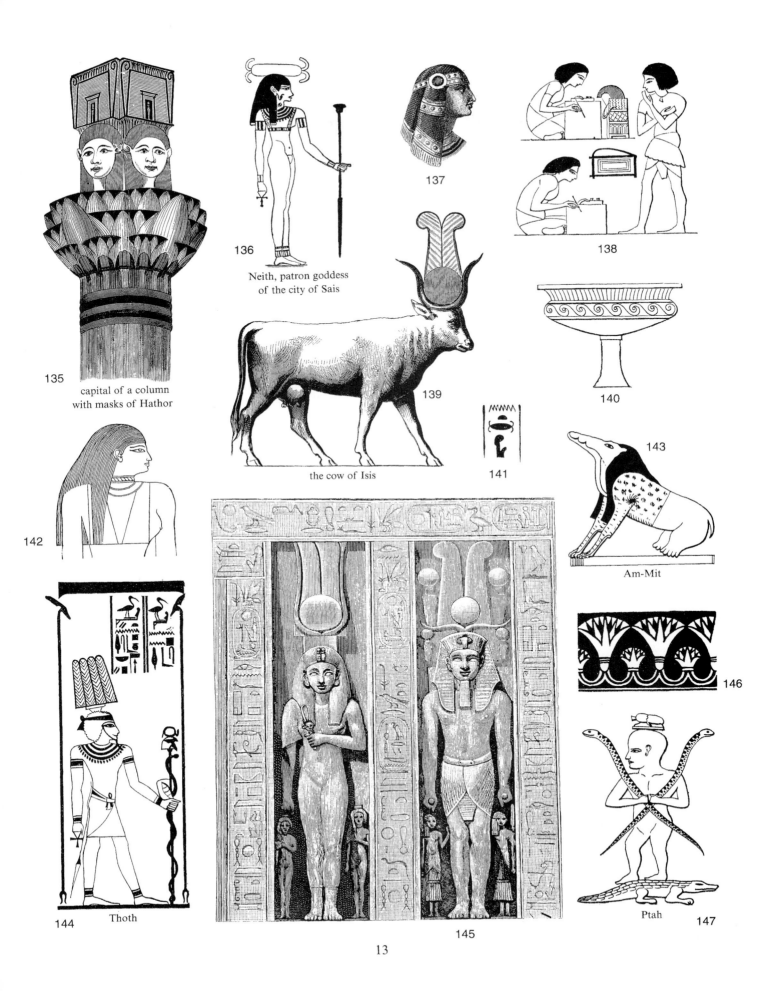

135
capital of a column
with masks of Hathor

136
Neith, patron goddess
of the city of Sais

137

138

139
the cow of Isis

140

141

142

143
Am-Mit

144   Thoth

145

146

Ptah   147

13

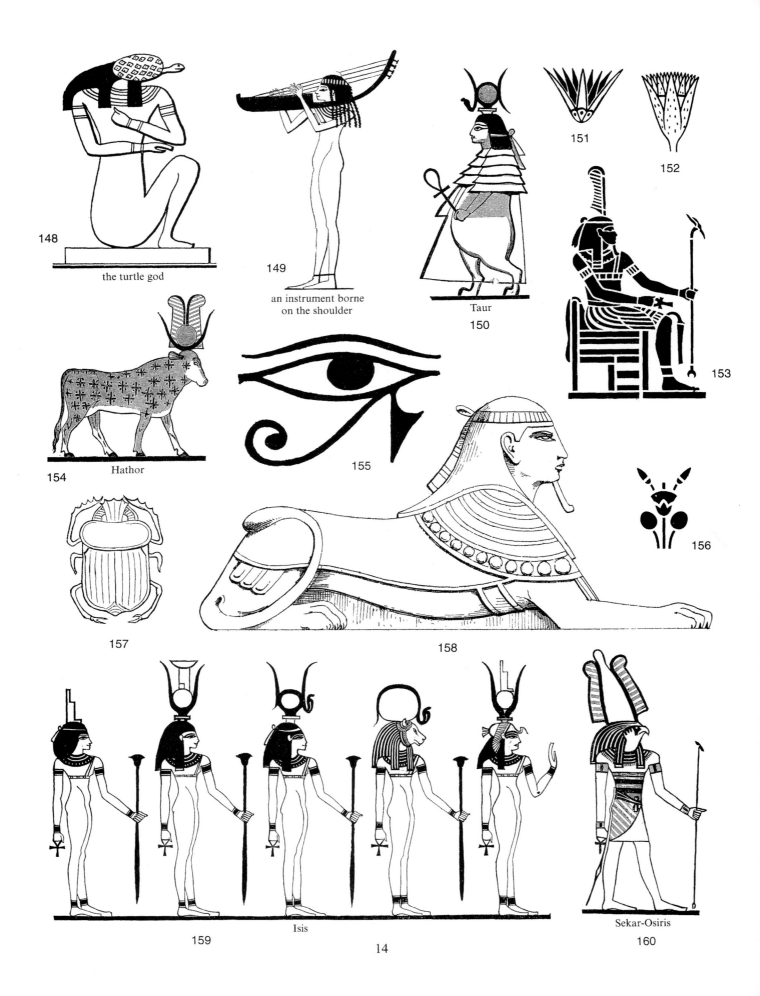

148

the turtle god

149

an instrument borne
on the shoulder

150

Taur

151

152

153

154

Hathor

155

156

157

158

159

Isis

160

Sekar-Osiris

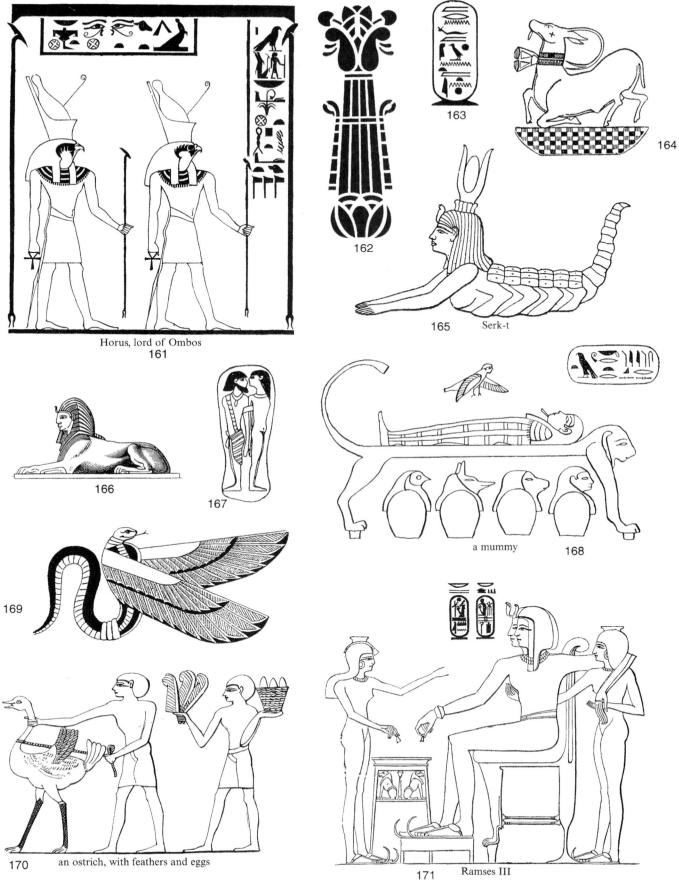

Horus, lord of Ombos
161

162

163

164

165   Serk-t

166

167

a mummy   168

169

170   an ostrich, with feathers and eggs

171   Ramses III

172

a sepulchral figure

a sphinx
173

174

175

double chair and single chair 176

177

a mummy's head, seen through open panel of coffin

178 King Tutankhamen on his throne

179

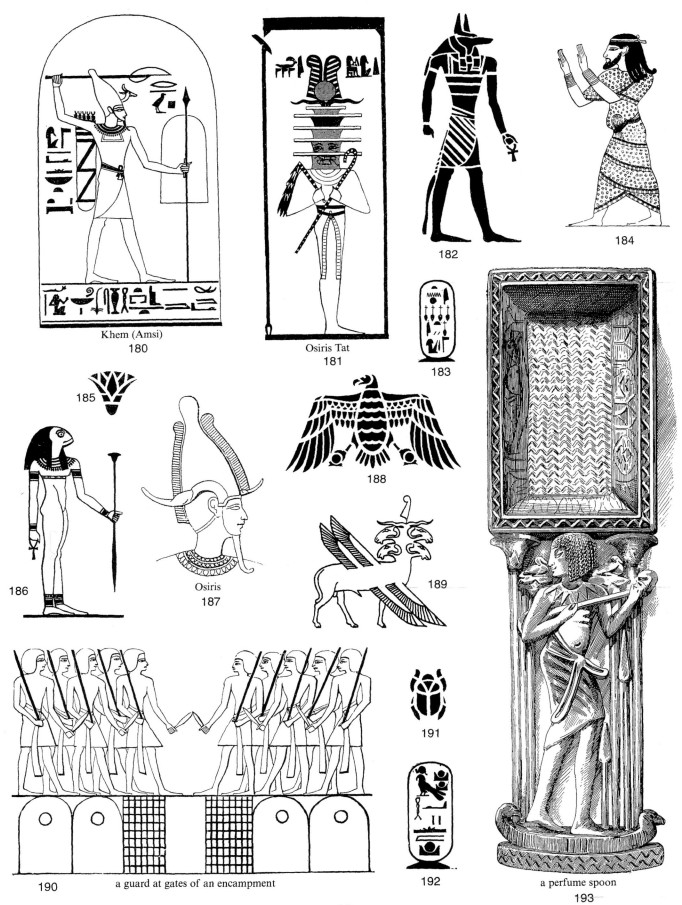

Khem (Amsi)
180

Osiris Tat
181

182

184

183

185

186

Osiris
187

188

189

190　　a guard at gates of an encampment

191

192

a perfume spoon
193

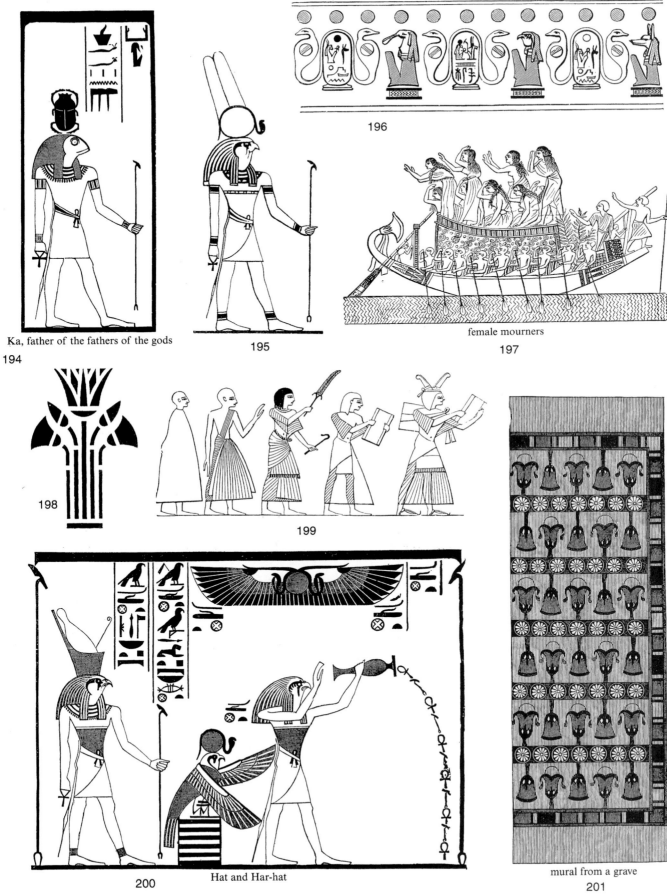

Ka, father of the fathers of the gods

194

195

196

female mourners

197

198

199

200   Hat and Har-hat

mural from a grave
201

Nebuu
202

Ta-aha
203

204

205

Nebhotep
206

Isis
207

208

209

Bast
210

211

212

213

214

Seti I anointing Khem (Amsi)

215

216

lyre ornamented with
carved animal head

217

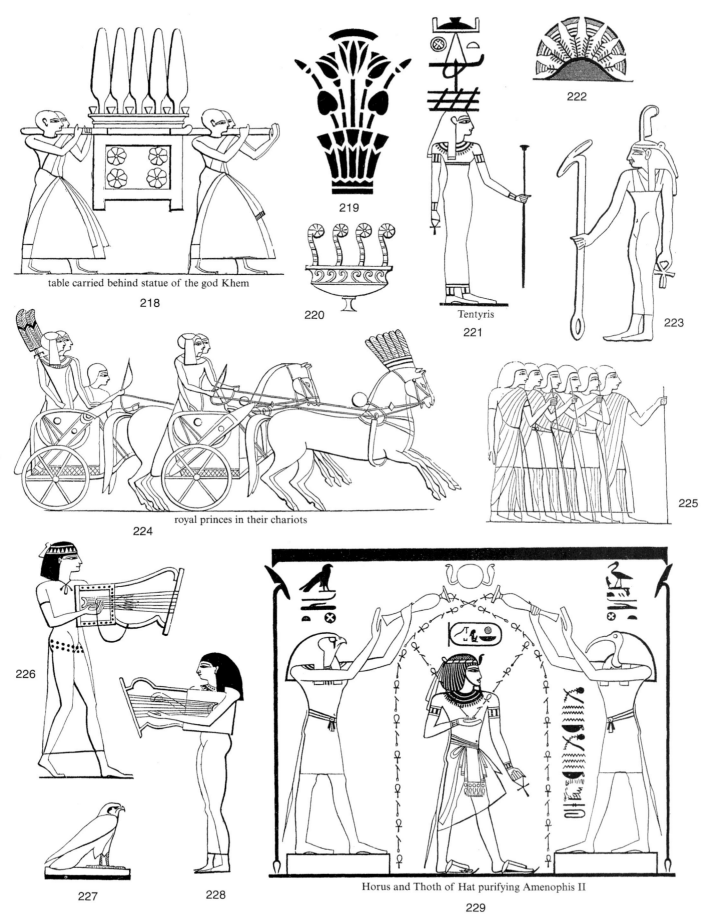

table carried behind statue of the god Khem

218

219

220

Tentyris

221

222

223

royal princes in their chariots

224

225

226

227

228

Horus and Thoth of Hat purifying Amenophis II

229

230

231

232

233

234

235
tying up onions for an offering

236
Uati, lady of heaven

237
Ptah-Sekar-Osiris

238
Cleopatra's needle

239

240
Cleopatra's needle

Kher heb   Smer   Sem   statue   Mesenti

241

242

243

scarab beetle   244

an ankh
245

246

247   248

249   headdress of a prince
250

251

sphinx

three representations of Neith
252

253

254

Asar (Osiris)   255

22

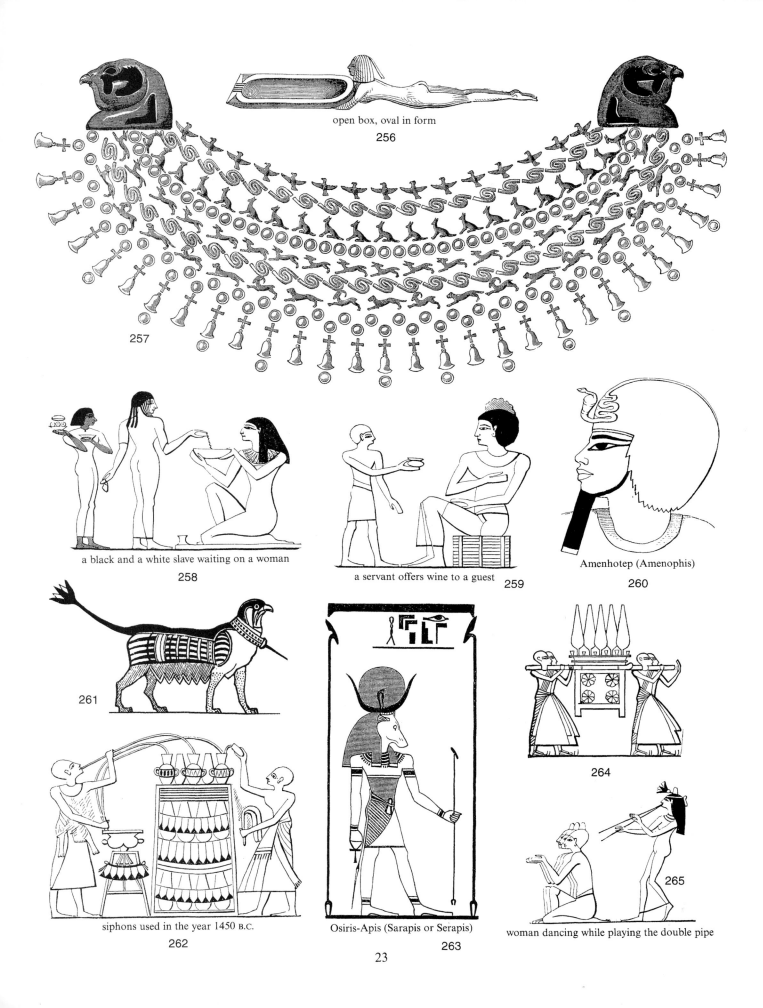

open box, oval in form
256

257

a black and a white slave waiting on a woman
258

a servant offers wine to a guest
259

Amenhotep (Amenophis)
260

261

siphons used in the year 1450 B.C.
262

Osiris-Apis (Sarapis or Serapis)
263

264

woman dancing while playing the double pipe
265

23

266
woman's headdress

267
a sepulchral figure
(frontal view)

268   Menephtah

MER·N·PTAH

MENEPH-
THES·

glass bottle
269

270

271
a stone scarab beetle with wide wings

272

Sati (Satis)
273

274
a sepulchral figure
(side view)

woman playing a guitar
275

lamentation for the dead
276

Uati

Nishem (the birth-goddess
Eileithyia)

Nubti

gestures of adoration

a group of women

musicians

winged gazelle

Amen-ra, king of the gods

25

a vase
290

Thutmose III,
protected by Buto, offers a pylon
291

292

293

294

Sat
295

Ras
296

297

298

299

Shu, the wind god
300

301

302

head of the god Bes

303

304

the goddess of truth with her eyes closed

306

winged solar disk

305

Osiris

307

Amon

308

As (Isis) winged

309

a harp raised on a stand

310

a servant aids her mistress

311

sculptors

312

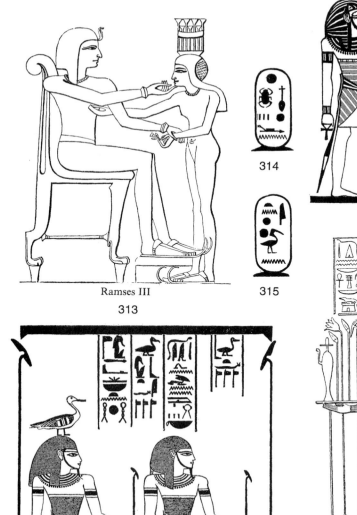

Ramses III

313

314

315

Ptah 316

317

318

319

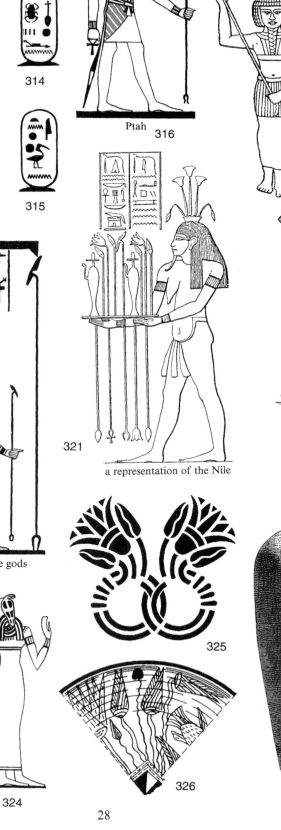

321

a representation of the Nile

a son of Ramses III

322

Geb (Seb), god of the earth and father of the gods

320

Sekhmet-Bast-Re

323

324

325

326

a sepulchral vase 327

28

328
Nut, goddess of the sky

329

330

331

332
queen with vulture headdress

333
a form of the goddess Neith

334

335

336

337

338
Bes and Hi

339
Sheshank (Shishak)

29

340

341

a row of archers
342

Ra-ta
343

kings wearing the crowns
of Upper and Lower Egypt
344

an ankh
345

346

347

348   Thoth and Safekh (goddess of history) write the name of Ramses II on fruits

349

30

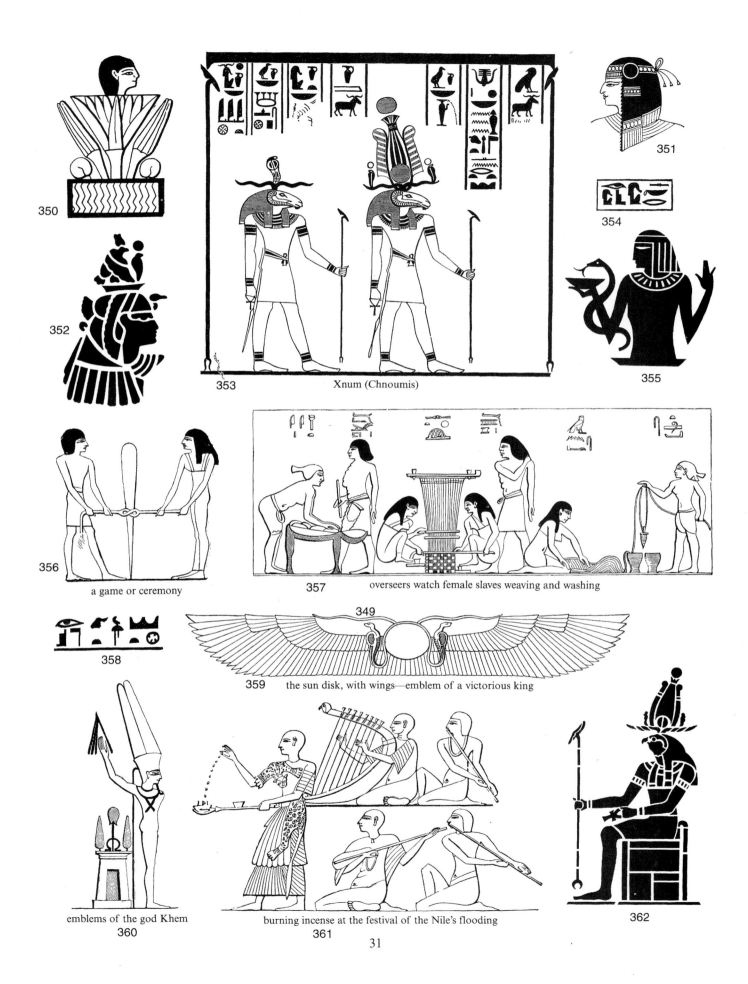

350

351

352

353   Xnum (Chnoumis)

354

355

356

a game or ceremony

357   overseers watch female slaves weaving and washing

358

349

359   the sun disk, with wings—emblem of a victorious king

emblems of the god Khem
360

burning incense at the festival of the Nile's flooding
361

362

31

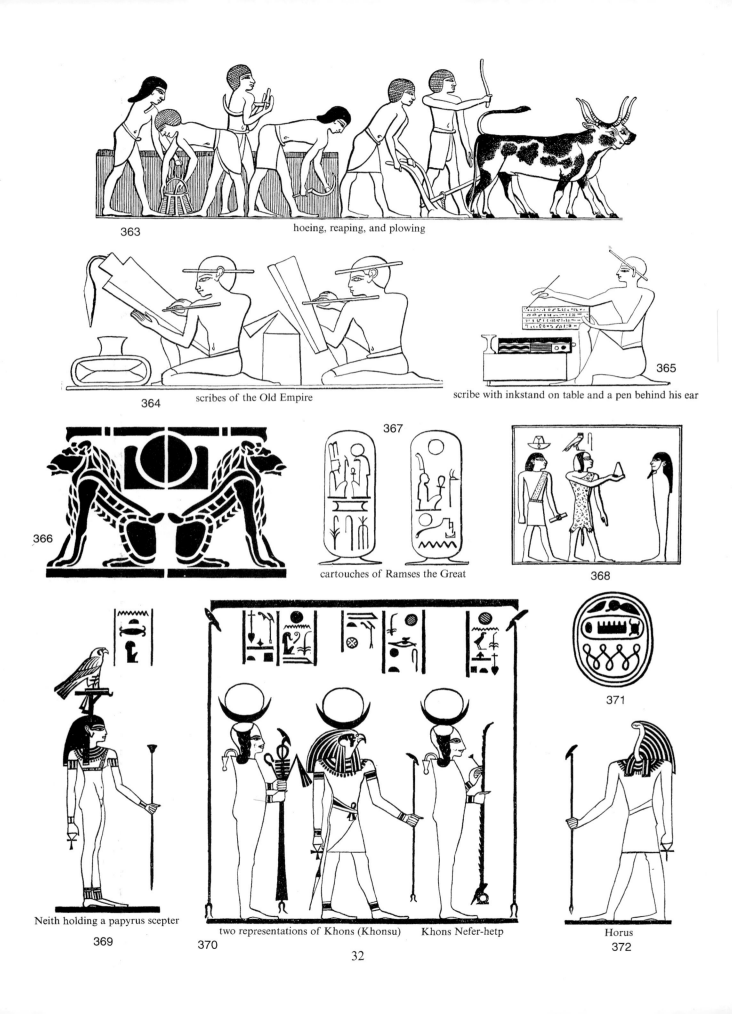

363   hoeing, reaping, and plowing

364   scribes of the Old Empire

365   scribe with inkstand on table and a pen behind his ear

366

367   cartouches of Ramses the Great

368

371

Neith holding a papyrus scepter

369

two representations of Khons (Khonsu)   Khons Nefer-hetp

370

Horus

372

32